Kayla Bean's Special Adventures

Kayla Bean Learns About Puberty

Daphne Olds
Logo by Winton Murrell Jr

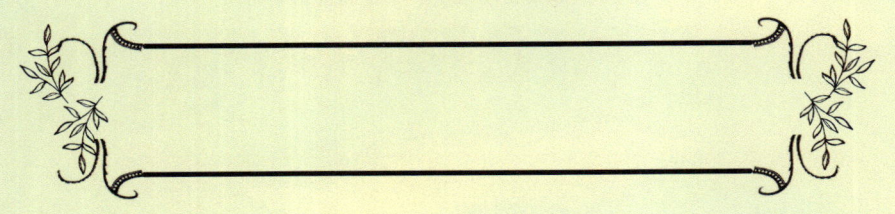

This book belongs to:

_____

Text © 2021 Daphne Olds
Logo © 2021 Winston Murrell Jr
Illustrations © Daphne Olds
All Rights Reserved

Kayla Bean's Special Adventures mini stories are dedicated to my beautiful daughter Makayla, aka Kayla Bean, my heartbeat. She is my number one inspiration in all that I do. As I often say, she is my daily blessing renewed. God gifted me with a special daughter who loves in a special way and I will forever be grateful for this blessing. Each day she teaches me her perspective of the world that we live in, and I must say, she definitely has the best view

--Daphne Olds (Johanna Dao)

Hi, my name is Kayla Bean. I want to share a story with you about a very important lesson I learned about my body. First, let me tell you a little about myself so you can understand why this story is so important to me.

I am 10 years old and I am apart of the Autism Spectrum Disorder community. Do you know what autism is? Autism is a set of developmental disorders that effects the way a person communicate and interact with others. That is just a general definition of it, there is much more to it. As a member of the community, I encourage you to learn as much as possible about it.

AUTISM ACCEPTANCE

My mom simply describes it as seeing the world through different glasses and having diffferent reactions to what we see because of those glasses.

For example, most people see the world through simple glasses such as theses. They are able to process everything they see normally with ease.

However, I see the world through glasses such as these. The world is a very colorful place for me and it takes me a while to process everything that I see. It also takes awhile for me to process things I hear, touch, and taste. This can effect the way I communicate.

Now that you know a little about me, let's get back to this important lesson that I learned about my body. This lesson is about me entering puberty and may be sensitive for some ears and eyes. So make sure your mom and dad are ok with you reading my story.

It all started one day while
I was taking a bath...

"Oh no! This can't be right. I have hair under my arms and on my girlie parts. Mommy, mommy, come quick! I need your help," Kayla Bean screams!

**(parents, please explain what girlie parts are to your child)

"What's wrong Kayla Bean? Did you hurt yourself?" asks mom.

"No mommy, but something is wrong with me. I have hair growing under my arms and on my girl parts," says Kayla Bean.

Kayla Bean's mom smiles and chuckles a little.

"It's not funny mommy," says Kayla Bean sadly. "All the kids are going to laugh at me."

"No. They are not going to laugh at you," says mom. "What is happening to you is normal. It happens to all kids as they are growing up into teenagers and young adults. It's called puberty. Once you get dressed, I will tell you more about it," mom explains.

After Kayla Bean is dressed, she finds her mom in the kitchen and mom begins to explain puberty to her.

"Kayla Bean, puberty is when your body goes through changes as you get older. It's preparing you to be an adult," said mom.

"What kind of changes?" Kayla Bean asked.

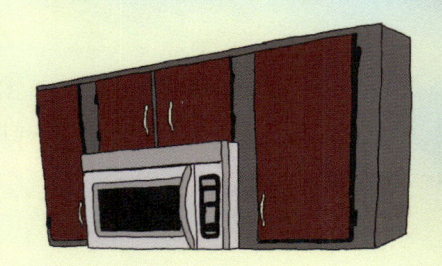

"Well you will begin to grow a little taller. Hair will start to grow under your arm and on your girlie parts and your voice will go through changes. You may also get tiny little pimples on your face called acne," mom explains.

"Wow, there are a lot changes with puberty," says Kayla Bean. "Do boys go through puberty too?"

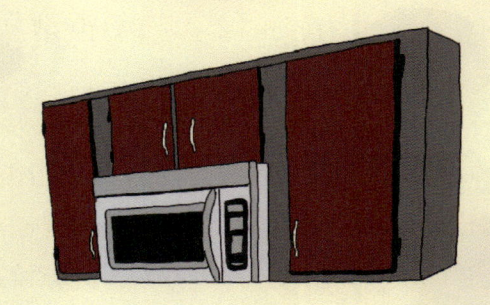

"Yes, Kayla Bean. Boys and girls go through puberty. Boys have changes to their bodies too," said mom.

"Wow, that's so cool mommy," says Kayla Bean.

"Yes, it is," said mom. "And the coolest part is that your body is changing to prepare you to become a mommy one day as an adult. As a young teenager, you will begin to experience what is called your menstrual cycle, also called a period," she explained.

"A period?" Kayla Bean asks confused. "Like the punctuation mark?" she asks. Kayla Bean's mom laughs lightly and begins to explain.

"No, not like the punctuation mark," mom explains. "It's an important physical change to your body that most girls experience in their early teenage years and all throughout adulthood," she tells Kayla Bean.

"Oh ok, mommy," says Kayla Bean. "Can you explain what a period is to me?"

"Yes," mom replies. "You and I will plan a mother-daughter day and I will explain what you need to know about your period," says mom. "That way you will be prepared when it happens. Now, let's get you ready for bed"

I dreamed all night about my mother-daughter day with my mom. I was so excited to learn more about my period.

Hi guys, this ends the story of how I learned about puberty! I hope you enjoyed it! If you want to know all the other things I have learned, please keep up with all my adventures. Thanks for reading! See you next time!

Questions for Mom and Dad

???

Do you have questions about puberty? Write down all questions that you would like for your parents to answer.

_____
_____
_____
_____
_____
_____
_____
_____
_____
_____
_____
_____
_____
_____

Questions for Mom and Dad

???

Do you have questions about puberty? Write down all questions that you would like for your parents to answer.

_____
_____
_____
_____
_____
_____
_____
_____
_____
_____
_____
_____
_____

KB Books Presents

Thank you for your interest in **KB Books Presents Kayla Bean's Special Adventures** series. Please check back frequently for new releases in the series coming soon.

Please check out our titles under planners and journals. We have a journal specifically designed to help individuals cope with their feelings, titled **KB Books Presents: In My Feelings**. It's the perfect gift for those who struggle with expressing their emotions. Just search for the title in the Amazon Marketplace or author pen name Johanna Dao or Daphne Olds

Visit us at:
www.kbbookspresents.com

Follow our KB Books Presents business pages on:

Facebook   Instagram

Printed in Great Britain
by Amazon